✂

Be of Good Heart

Joseph McSorley

Be of Good Heart

Sustaining Christian Hope
in Our Difficult Days

SOPHIA INSTITUTE PRESS®
Manchester, New Hampshire

Be of Good Heart: Sustaining Christian Hope in Our Difficult Days is an abridged edition of *Be of Good Heart: A Plea for Christian Optimism* (New York: P. J. Kenedy and Sons, 1924). This 1999 edition by Sophia Institute Press contains minor editorial revisions to the original text.

Sophia Institute Press®
Box 5284, Manchester, NH 03108
1-800-888-9344
www.sophiainstitute.com

Nihil obstat: Arthur J. Scanlan, S.T.D., *Censor Librorum*
Imprimatur: Patrick Cardinal Hayes, Archbishop of New York
New York, August 28, 1924

Library of Congress Cataloging-in-Publication Data

McSorley, Joseph, b. 1874.
    [Be of good heart. Selections]
    Be of good heart : sustaining Christian hope in our difficult
    days / Joseph McSorley.
        p. cm.
    Includes bibliographical references.
    ISBN 0-918477-91-3 (pbk. : alk. paper)
    1. Christian life — Catholic authors. 2. Consolation. I. Title.
BX2350.2.M38825   1999
242'.4 — DC21   98-55717 CIP

99 00 01 02 03   10 9 8 7 6 5 4 3 2 1

Contents

Editor's Note: The biblical references in the following pages are based on the Douay-Rheims edition of the Old and New Testaments. Where applicable, quotations have been cross-referenced with the numeration in the Revised Standard Version, using the following symbol: (RSV =).

Be of Good Heart

Chapter One

❧

Why You Should Be Hopeful

✢

Hope sustains you

O soul, too quickly despondent, too easily cast down, listen to the comforting word of the great apostle: "We are saved by hope."[1]

It is a rallying cry, a trumpet call, turning defeat into victory. Inspired, inspiring, it awakens a sense of danger, arouses new energy, directs our efforts. Hope is in truth our need; without it, we are lost.

Too often, when we step across the threshold into the beginning of a new period of life, as at the new year or upon a birthday, we find ourselves confronted by solemn, even saddening thoughts. Like other years that have passed, this coming year will doubtless be a time of trial and struggle; and already we feel an uneasy foreboding as to its mysterious content. We look out as a mariner upon an uncharted ocean; we face forward as soldiers on the

---

[1] Rom. 8:24.

eve of battle, thinking of the morrow, whose sunset we may never see. Other years, opening like this one, have brought suffering such as we pray God we may never endure again. Men have faced a new year as we face this, and before its close, they have gone down to crushing defeat and everlasting ruin.

These reflections make the threshold of a year an ominous thing. Around it gather suggestions of unmeasured, and therefore dreadful, dangers. We throw back a glance at the disappointments of the past; we peer uncertainly into the future, and not improbably we are overcome with gloom.

Will it really be worthwhile, this year that is beginning? Will these approaching months add to the sum total of our happiness? Can we watch the course of days and weeks as they commence to flow and welcome them as a divine opportunity? Or must we enter upon this year without confidence and without enthusiasm, as men who have no hope?

These are important and very practical questions. And most of us who venture to answer them must acknowledge that we are advancing toward the future with much too faint a heart and with far too weak a courage.

Why You Should Be Hopeful

True, this is an age of initiative, and we live in the reign of assurance and self-confidence. People are aggressive and energetic and resourceful and venturesome nowadays; they are restless and quick and ambitious. And our own nation may be said to have attained a sort of preeminence in these characteristics; at any rate, no one charges us with lagging very far behind the leaders. Our men are vigorous; our women are self-reliant; the thoughts we think and the deeds we do are daring. Hardly in any respect are we regarded as timid or diffident or backward.

Yet, curiously enough, and almost as if by way of compensation for our excess of alertness in other respects, we lie open to the charge of a certain sluggishness and faintheartedness with regard to supernatural opportunities. Observers whose experience is wide and whose discernment is fine, affirm that the tendency to spiritual discouragement is widespread among us; that, in things of the soul, we easily become downcast and depressed; that we are hypersensitive and exceedingly timid; and that, for the most part, we habitually face the future in a fearful and cowardly mood.

Worldly people there are who, by dint of persistent attempts, succeed in keeping their attention distracted from the perils about to come. They feel no apprehension about the issue of a struggle, to whose approach they do not even advert. But the more serious-minded are often perturbed, as they perceive themselves to be entering upon another division of life, drifting so steadily, so inevitably toward the grave, still with untrimmed lamps, still with empty hands.

One year has been so like another. Confirmed in habits that are wrong, and set in ways that are evil, we have gone so far that now nothing short of a divine assurance of better things can dispel the nightmare of despondency, or erase the paralyzing memory of our fruitless, inglorious struggles.

Despondency is widespread. Yet such a temper of mind is anything but wise, anything but healthy, anything but Christian. The outlook of the religious man ought to be that of one whose footsteps lead along the fortunate pathway of Providence and beside the inviting fields of opportunity.

Reasons for hope are all around you
See! From each coming day shines the gleam of a coming blessing; with each morning's sun there rise new

reasons for confidence in the promise given. God is good; He is mighty; His interests are inseparable from ours; His knowledge and His strength are lent to us to be employed in our service. Christ is the light of the world.[2] To everyone believing in Him, He is the sunshine of eternal day. Since He has come, "hope springs eternal in the human breast";[3] joy and peace and the glad assurance of everlasting rest are the portion of all who enroll themselves as His disciples.

The future is filled with promise

The true significance of each opening year is that it has come out of eternity to bear to us immeasurable blessings; and as we look forward into each span of time, we perceive some fresh evidence of its divine possibilities. Each year will leave us farther along the road to Heaven, wrought more closely into the likeness of our Divine Exemplar. This is God's plan. It will be carried out if we do not interfere with it. Therefore is our courage high and our heart full of hope. We actually expect eternal

---

[2] John 8:12, 9:5.
[3] Alexander Pope, "An Essay on Man," Epistle 1, line 95.

happiness to be our lot, and the reflection of that visioned future may be detected shining in the countenance of every Christian saint.

For us, then, this year is a time of promise. We should begin each day with the high spirit of dauntless courage, never with quaking heart. God has promised, and that promise cannot be made void. All that we need will be provided. We shall advance; we shall conquer; we shall be guarded against every evil. Nothing shall happen to the least of us — not disappointment or sickness or failure or fault — that the Lord God will not make to work together for good. Such, in very truth, is the proper outlook of the Christian.

It is a way of looking at things that, for its justification, has only to appeal to what our faith in God implies. The purpose of creation — was it not that God might raise us to a divine intimacy with Him? And His relation to us — has it ever been, can it ever be, other than that of a father working ceaselessly for the perfecting of the children whom he tenderly loves? The attributes with which we clothe the divine nature make other conceptions than this impossible. God is lovingly and wisely kind; He is gracious and sweet and compassionate and patient.

Read the history of His dealings with men — even with sinful men — and mark the vindication of the claim that there is no end to the mercy of God, no limit to His love. Turn to that dearest revelation of the divine nature: the visible life of Jesus Christ. At once you see the sufficient reason of the Christian's quenchless hope. That Christ should tell the divine story of the prodigal;[4] that He should make a saint of a Magdalene;[5] that, in the last hour of His dying agony, He should open the gates of Paradise to a sinner just beginning his repentance[6] — these things convince us that if we trust Him to the very end, we shall make no mistake.

But better than all this is the assurance that each of us can find within his own soul. Glance back at the past, and recall the patience and the gentleness and the love of our Father as manifested in His words of pardon, forgiveness, and comfort to the conscience when, weary with sin or broken with sorrow, we have turned to Him. Does not the very memory of it make us feel that we need never fear, need never question His attitude toward us?

[4] Luke 15:11-32.
[5] Cf. Luke 7:37-48.
[6] Luke 23:42.

Be of Good Heart

Hope is essential to your well-being

Were there required further confirmation of this belief, we should be able to find it in the actual constitution
of the human soul. Hope and confidence are essential to
our spiritual well-being. It is impossible to accomplish
anything with a soul in which the tide of trust is ever at
an ebb, in which the prevailing temper is one of doubt
and fretfulness and anxiety. Confidence enters essentially
into the chances of success of a soldier marching to the
field of battle, of a wrestler leaping forward to the struggle, of an athlete preparing to run in the race. But much
more needful is it in the progress of a soul toward the goal
of its highest ambition: Heaven.

No less in religion than in therapeutics — or, rather,
much more in the former than in the latter — we recog-
nize that hope is both an element and a condition of
healthiness, and that an expectation of success must
quicken the heart of him who is to triumph over his enemies. It is in the supernatural as in the natural order, for
the religious process is not altogether unlike the physical.
What enthusiasm is to the youth, and ambition to the
apprentice, and peace of mind to the invalid, such is

hope to the Christian. And just as the characteristic that makes a soldier famous is not to know when he is beaten, so the sentiment that saves a Christian is to believe that God's sufficient help will never be withheld from his will so long as it is struggling, however feebly, toward the good.

In season and out of season, this truth has been preached by the Church, which, through the centuries, continues to be the great spiritual teacher of the world. Where does she rank hope? Beside faith and charity, as one of that inseparable trinity of virtues without which no man comes to life eternal. The lesson is impressive. No one believes in God as he should, unless a firm hope is united to his faith. No one loves God as he should, unless, together with love, there is found in his soul such trust as will cast out fear.[7] When all else has been out-grown, there must yet remain these three: faith, hope, and charity. And although, indeed, the greatest of these is charity,[8] we must never allow ourselves to forget that one of them is hope.

---

[7] Cf. 1 John 4:18.
[8] 1 Cor. 13:13.

Be of Good Heart

As the obligation to hope is a duty too often neglected, so likewise the nature of hope is a matter very frequently misunderstood; the ways and means of fostering hope within the soul seemingly remain unknown to many.

Now, to hope is to expect, to await, to look forward trustfully to the approach of a blessing that one counts upon. In religion, it is an expectation of the blessing of eternal life and of the means necessary to obtain it. The Christian whose heart is right expects to be saved; he expects to make progress toward perfection. We need not, at the present moment, insist upon the fact that a rational hope necessarily implies a resolution to be faithful in the discharge of duties and the fulfillment of obligations. That is plain. But the resolution to be faithful must be supplemented by a confidence that will reinforce one's decision to serve God.

All this seems to imply that there is a part to be played by the will in the maintaining of a hopeful state of soul — and this is exactly the point that needs to be insisted upon before all others. People are apt to regard hope as an infused virtue in too strict and exclusive a sense, to assume that grace does all and the will does nothing in producing hopefulness — just as, in the natural order, they assume cheerfulness to be entirely a matter of temperament, overlooking the achievements of those who, by persevering effort, have first checked and then mastered an emotional tendency to pessimism or despair. The truth is that a man's deliberate choice has a very important function in determining his mental outlook. Hence, to a considerable extent, every man is responsible for his attitude toward the future.

Which of us really appreciates this as he should? Most are quick to perceive and conscientious to confess faults against the virtue of faith and charity, but few advert to the possibility of committing sin by perversity or sluggishness of will in the matter of hope. Yet there it is: an act to be practiced and a virtue to be acquired with the help of a grace that is never wanting.

One may easily sin against hope, then. How? Why, how else but by willfully dwelling on things that discourage us; by indulging the temptation to tolerate, if not actually to entertain, the devils of moodiness and depression and melancholy and sadness; by refusing to take such measures — physical, mental, and religious — as will help us throw off sentiments no less favorable to sin than weakening to virtue.

Faith healing and Christian Science may be the cloak of many a foolishness, the cover of many a sham, and the excuse of many an exaggeration, but there is one truth to which these systems hold fast: the good old truth that for the man whose will is right, there are no real evils; that to such as love God, "all things work together unto good."[9] In fact, it is an elementary teaching of the Church that, by God's grace, the will can expel and overcome all the real evils by which man is afflicted and, what is more, can convert every one of them into a blessing.

You must develop a spirit of hope

Practically, then, how shall we assist and cooperate with grace in the matter of acquiring the spirit of hope? We smile, perhaps, when we are told that one of the means is to keep as sane and as healthy as possible. We know that to waste or to abuse the strength of body or mind is wicked. Do we not also know that among the penalties with which the God of nature visits those who disregard His common laws are the nervous and emotional disturbances that bring on continued or periodic depression

---

[9] Rom. 8:28.

and moodiness and hopelessness? We may perhaps have recognized that this holds true of the greater and grosser sins. The question is whether we quite appreciate the degree of our responsibility in the finer and more subtle yielding of our wills to the attractions of selfishness.

This, then, is one of the things we can do — namely, inhibit the excessive consideration of the dark and depressing aspects of life. Further, we can contribute positively to the cultivation of a hopeful temper by retaining before our soul's eye, with such permanency as we can achieve, those holy and comforting truths which are the basis of confidence in the future.

A little reflection will convince us that this implies more prayer and less introspection; a looking often at God and seldom at ourselves. Thus we shall soon accustom our minds to contemplate the goodness of the divine nature, the infinite extent of God's mercy, and the loveliness of His works. And we shall cease to dwell in a world where we occupy the central place and where our interests are supreme, and walk instead in the company of those whose eyes and minds are fixed lastingly upon God.

Two types of religious men there are, with distinctive traits well defined: the fearful and the hopeful. It is surely

unnecessary to state which one of them possesses the better chance of victory under stress of temptation.
The ideal Christian type has ever included something of the childlike — a face that turns toward God as toward a trusted parent; a smile that lasts through the greatest trials and most threatening dangers; a heart that throbs with perfect trust in the goodness of the Father; a spirit that realizes that, although the measure of human frailty may be great, the measure of divine mercy is infinitely more; a spirit that rests upon God as a son in his father's arms, as a babe on the bosom of his mother.

As we enter upon each new year, therefore, let it be with high-hearted hope. Here it is before us, a God-given opportunity. This span of days and the experiences that it is to bring have been planned by Providence as a means of grace and blessing to us. Despite all failure in the past, then, we will believe that the coming year is full of good for us; that pleasant and unpleasant things, duties hard and duties easy, trials and sorrows and temptations and surprises and disappointments and apparent failures will prove to be God's means of bringing us to that final victory which above all other goods we most heartily desire.

Chapter Two

God Is Always Near

God has come among us

Why was Christ born? To bring God and man together. Magnificently was that purpose fulfilled. Here, in this common world, a Man among men, Christ dwelt visibly. He grew and labored; He spoke and suffered. A Man from Heaven — God among men.

Forever, after the sight of Him, there was stamped upon the imagination of the race an ineffaceable image of perfection. Twisted inextricably into the fibers of the human heart were new cords of strength and patience and supernatural holiness. God had come nearer than ever before; and, in consequence, man was to be for all time greater than ever before.

The history of Christian civilization demonstrates this. For all its gloom of shadow and its many streaks of blood, for all its disappointing blindness and hardness, for all its lead-footed following of heroic leadership and its headlong rush into each new field of gluttony and of

lust — for all this, Christian society, down through
the ages, displays the ever-present influence of a divine
ideal. It shows the blending of God's thoughts and
actions with those of men. It proves that Christ never
abandoned the race He undertook at any price to save;
that He is among us in every time and place; that He is
with us here and now. The best that is recorded in the
human story, the finest achievements of civilization
disclose, like threads of gold, deeds of divine brightness
warped through the darker woof and making a pattern
fairer than anything the mind of man could imagine in
an eternity.

Since Christ came, it has been a different world and
a different life. Love and marriage are ennobled; birth
and death are glorified. The hard tasks that daily fall to
labor's lot are softened and sanctified. The care of little
ones, the training of the young, and the pursuit of knowledge have become divine vocations; they are among the
hallowed things that men and women reverence. We
gather for common worship around a Sacrificial Altar
and a Table of Mystery, where Christ again is offered up
to save from sin, and Christ's Body again is broken like
bread for souls to feed upon.

All through the ranks of the uncounted millions who have taken to themselves the livery of His Name, there is recognized, now clearly and now dimly, yet universally, an ideal of human relationship that is unique. Bonded by some sort of indescribable fellowship, driven by an unnamed inspiration, men and women accept as an inevitable duty the burden of human service. It is a conception that dawns gradually and, in some respects, slowly. Generations may deny it, and individuals may reject it, but, in the end, it makes itself felt as the necessary consequence of being a Christian. On it goes, widening, deepening the channel of human sympathies, until human love, made pure by the touch of Christ in passing, has flowed into the farthest, murkiest recesses of misery. And lepers, idiots, drunkards, and criminals, who have been rescued, rise up and call Him blessed.

Yes! It is scarcely to be denied by the historian: the social order of the Christian world is permeated, illumined, and energized by a force, a light, a power that, in some mysterious, inexplicable way, comes and goes with the coming and going of Christianity. It is the presence of Christ making itself felt in the world. But, although the traces of His passing are too plain to be ignored, although the world is forever different and better now, still, in each individual life, the process of improvement must forever recommence, and in many an individual life, little has yet been done.

Faith allows you to live in God's presence

What may be hoped for by each is suggested in the prayer breathed by St. Paul, as he thinks of the needs of his dear Ephesians: "That Christ may dwell by faith in your hearts."[10] These words present an ideal of what the life of the Christian should be. It should be a life spent with God. Every moment and every activity, all thought and endurance, all impulse and determination, the earning of one's daily bread, the strife against recurrent temptation, the grief at great bereavement, physical pain and sorrow and joy, strenuous fighting and exultant victory, tender communion and stern performance of heart-breaking duties — none of these should be apart from God.

Into the grand harmony of the Christian's whole life should be introduced the music of Christ's participation,

[10] Eph. 3:17.

divinely beautiful, strengthening, dominating. In nothing that he does can the Christian be quite as other men.

The fulfilling of this idea of constant communion and harmonious cooperation with the divine presence is a gift of God; it depends upon a generous grace of His, which we can never do enough to deserve. But it implies another element, too, for the bestowing of the gift is conditioned by the attitude we assume and the response we make. This aspect of the matter needs to be considered very carefully. What is the proper attitude for us to assume when God draws near? What can be done? What must we do?

St. Paul has hinted the answer in one word of his: faith. We should have faith. And faith is a gift that we must stretch out our hands to receive; it approaches, like a divine guest whom we go forth to meet and strive heartily to entertain. Faith is at the beginning of holiness. It is the root, indispensable to the growing and the budding and the blossoming of that fair flower whose fragrance should be wafted through the garden of our lives. If Christ is going to dwell at all within us, He will begin to dwell by faith.

Faith includes, of course, implicitly or explicitly, every single truth that God has ever taught, or will ever teach.

But the particular point of faith that may well be emphasized in connection with the matter now under consideration is belief in the omnipresence of God.

In every nook and corner of this visible world, in the midst of the big and little things that make up the daily lives of men and women, at every moment and in every sort of situation, God is near to us, looking upon us, sounding the depths of our consciousness. He is appealing to us, and He is sensitive to our response, to our good conduct or our ill-doing. This is, indeed, the greatest fact of human life, and constant attention to this fact is the substructure of the greatest possible human holiness.

To believe in the constant presence of the God who loves us and who, for love's sake, lays a law upon us — to believe in this and to act consistently with such belief, is the most practical general rule of holy living that can be devised. The cultivation of faith in God's omnipresence and the endeavor to behave in a fashion consistent with this faith is, then, the beginning of the preparation for that ideal life of which St. Paul speaks. This, and this alone, will bring us to that state wherein Christ will dwell in our hearts.

You can develop a sense of God's presence

To promote this sense of the presence of God, we should make the spirit of reverence habitual. It helps much if we can bring ourselves always to act as if we were within the sanctuary. This is not to say that we are forbidden to rest and relax, to laugh and amuse ourselves; but it is to say that under the surface should be the permanent sense of being in the presence of God. Often, by a word, or even by mere aspiration, a prayer will be offered to the ever-present Lover. Temptation will acquire something of the horror of a desecration, a sacrilege.

To keep hold of the great truth, to refuse to let ourselves be drawn away by the vain argument and the fallacy of lying appearances that imply that there is no God — this is the beginning of the holiness that ensures happiness. Remember that great central truth of life, and the remembrance will prepare your soul perfectly for God's best gifts.

Again, we must strive not only to be aware that God is present, but also to act as if His interests were supreme in life. The usual tendency of nature is to put material goods in the first place and to rank other people after ourselves. We must go straight against this tendency if we would be a fit habitation for the indwelling Christ.

It is not hard to see how different our lives would soon become if the chief fact of consciousness were the omnipresence of God. It would mean, first of all, the possession of a spirit of prayer.

Prayer is not confined to spoken communication; it is not limited to one or two of the sentiments possible to the human heart. Prayer is well described as conversation with God. How could one be ever conscious of God's presence, and yet refrain from frequent communication with Him? It might concern the great crises of one's life, or the trifling matters of a common day; it might be a petition for the things we need, or thanksgiving for precious favors already received; it might voice the agonized sense of desolation in a soul terribly tried, or the quiet adoration of one telling God simply, "It is good to be here." But at all times and in all places, the soul would be aware that God is within reach of every creature that cries to Him, even in unspoken whispers; and its deep sentiment would be communicated to the closest and dearest Friend, whose sympathy is as certain as His power to help is great.

And it is not hard to see that, almost inevitably, advertence to this dominating presence would lead to a transmutation of values in our appraisal of things and deeds. The shining baubles of the world look lusterless enough to a man familiar with the radiance of Christ's beauty. Ways of dealing that the world approves of, and that we ourselves once admired, shrivel up into pettiness and meanness if we consider how they appear to God. The custom of driving sharp bargains in shop and market seems impossibly barbaric when we remember that Christ, who erected such different rules of conduct for His disciples, is here present, waiting to see whether we are loyal of heart or base traitors. In one word, if we remember that God is looking at us, we are very apt to behave as God wishes.

The soul that trains itself by this method, sooner or later, will receive the blessing that Paul invoked upon the Ephesians: "May Christ dwell by faith in your hearts."

Chapter Three

⚛

God Asks Only
One Thing of You

✧

The greatest law is the law of love

It was a critical moment in the history of the world when the lawyer, rising up, asked our divine Lord the question: "Which is the great commandment?"[11]

So much that is vital in the eternal interests of mankind depended upon the answer. The words about to fall from the lips of Christ would determine the fate of uncounted millions. For His answer was to reveal the divine standard of measurement, was to make plain forever by what rule a man's life is tested on the Day of Judgment, was to tell us in what things to place our hope of eternal life and give us an imperishable picture of what, in the mind of God, a perfect human soul should be.

Our Savior replies quickly to the question. The momentous answer is given in two short phrases that impart the very essence of the spirit of His gospel and, like an

[11] Matt. 22:36.

33

all-inclusive revelation, sum up the contents of the whole law, disclosing in a flash the most precious element in the relationship of God with man. Henceforward there can be no mistake: the kingdom of God is the kingdom of love.

The spirit of selfishness is excluded, forever excluded and utterly condemned. The one condition that ensures a man's admission to the divine kingdom and guarantees his portion of eternal life is whole-hearted, whole-souled love of God and God's children. "The great commandment is this: Thou shalt love the Lord thy God. And the second is like to it: Thou shalt love thy neighbor as thyself. On these two commandments depend the whole Law and the prophets."[12]

How it rang through the world, that divine proclamation of the law of love by the lips of Jesus Christ, echoing back into the dim ages of pre-Christian history as if to summon from the dead those nameless and unremembered spirits who, in their lifetime, fulfilled this law; flinging into far countries and among undiscovered peoples a revelation that the chance of eternal life was also theirs;

[12] Cf. Matt. 12:37-40.

rolling endlessly down the centuries to point out the certain way of holiness to all human generations ever to be born! It made no exception, and it allowed no excuse, this ruling of the Son of God on the question that concerned His Father's law — a heart-filling, soul-absorbing love of God would imply admission to the heavenly kingdom, even if angels had to guide the perfect lover there.

Once, in the school of an imperfect revelation, emphasis had been laid upon obedience inspired by fear, the tribute of a creature to its Creator. Now the partial illumination, become an all-revealing light, showed Heaven and earth in their true relation and orientated man to God in the perfect attitude of obedience inspired by love.

Guided by this light, men and women were to scale the heights of a holy mountain upon whose summit God awaited them, and were to be admitted to the privileges of an intimacy of affection never imagined possible. And love was to be the all-sufficing condition of this divine bestowal.

Love is all God asks of you

Love suffices. Race does not matter any more, nor tribe, nor family. Strength and learning shall not avail to save; weakness and ignorance and poverty shall never disqualify. Having fulfilled the one condition of whole-hearted love, the fisherman shall be greater than the scholar and the peasant higher than the king. Even past and repented sin shall be no obstacle, for among the wonderful saints of God are numbered many who, after years wasted in the paths of sin's lowest hell, cast off self-ishness at last and became great lovers, valiantly begin-ning their painful climb to the far heights of divine union.

It is extremely difficult for the human mind to under-stand that what God asks of us is simply to love Him. We look high up into the heavens and afar to the ends of the earth, wondering what extraordinary thing we can do in order to win the supreme prize of eternal life. We find it almost beyond belief that what the Lord requires is love and the things that love implies. Perhaps because it is so hard for us to realize, the doctrine is repeated over and over again in the pages of the New Testament. Our Sav-ior assures the Magdalene that "many sins are forgiven her, because she hath loved much."[13] To the scribe

---

[13] Luke 7:47.

affirming the necessity of love, He says, "Thou art not far from the kingdom of God."[14] St. Jude receives the promise: "He that loveth me shall be loved by my Father."[15] Thus often repeated by our Savior, the same truth is affirmed by St. Paul, and still more frequently by St. John.

Borne in upon the human consciousness by the insistence and the ceaseless repetition of the Gospel teaching, love inspired the new type of holiness that characterizes Christian saints. Whatever other gifts they did or did not possess, whatever other quality set them apart from the common run of men, one thing was unmistakably theirs: love, whole-hearted and supreme.

Down through the centuries, a divinely appointed agency preserved the spirit of Christ's teaching. The men and women schooled by the Catholic Church shared that same exalted conception of the worth of love that marked the first disciples of Christ and the pupils of Paul and John. If there is any error that would seem to be quite impossible for a Christian to make, it is the folly of

[14] Mark 12:34.
[15] John 14:21.

attempting to replace love with any substitute, of imagining that great learning or lip-service or magnificent works can ever have the value of simple love.

Yet, at times, here and there, Christians have gone astray. Implicitly, no doubt unconsciously, a Christian will deny the supremacy of love by concentrating attention exclusively upon the other elements of religion, exercising care to excel in other qualities, measuring nearness to the kingdom of Heaven by some other attribute or some other achievement. Often, and often in the history of the worship of God, has this gross mistake been made. It has been made by you and me.

For true love comes not naturally or easily to us who are selfish first by instinct, and then largely by habit, too. We are so much less ready to give than to get. We think it most blessed to receive. We exchange and calculate and barter more contentedly than we give away. We are loath to cast off self-interest and, for love's sake, to undertake the great adventure of abandoning all our substance and counting it as nothing.

How often we manifest this spirit of selfishness! When, for instance, temptation confronts us and promises us disloyalty's rich reward, how blind we are to the

better worth of simple love. How frequently, surrendering
basely to the attack of greedy avarice or storming passion
or furious hate, we equivalently repudiate and abandon
love, deny the truth that Jesus affirmed, follow a false
gospel, offer allegiance to the antichrist, and discredit
the ideal for which our Savior died.

Against such a mistake, such a betrayal, we must be
on our guard. High and clear before our eyes let the fact
of love's supremacy be set. Love is the one thing needful.[16]
For love is the supreme ideal, the great commandment of
the Christian law.

Love of God calls for love of neighbor
And with love of God must coexist love of neighbor.
The questioning lawyer received a twofold answer that —
to our astonishment — sets the love of man alongside the
love of God so that the holy soul may no more exclude
the one than the other. Heartily accepted, this doctrine
would remake the world.

This teaching re-echoes throughout the pages of St.
John and St. Paul. John's ceaseless exhortation, "Little

[16] Cf. Luke 10:42.

children, love one another,"[17] and Paul's flaming words in his first letter to the Corinthians,[18] preach the same truth: the excellence of love over every other gift. A practical result of this doctrine was the extraordinary affection of the early Christians for one another, a phenomenon so striking that the very pagans marveled at the depth and sincerity and constancy of their love.

How plainly is the love of our neighbor made the actual test of our love of God. "By this shall all men know that you are my disciples: that you have love one for another."[19] "Bear ye one another's burdens, and so ye shall fulfill the law of Christ."[20] "He that loveth his brother abideth in the light."[21] "We know that we have passed from death to life because we love the brethren."[22] "If any man say, 'I love God' and hateth his brother, he is a liar."[23]

---

[17] Cf. 1 John 3:11.
[18] 1 Cor. 13:1-13.
[19] John 13:35.
[20] Gal. 6:2.
[21] 1 John 2:10.
[22] 1 John 3:14.
[23] 1 John 4:20.

Yet, with all Christ's insistence upon His new commandment that we love one another even as He loves us,[24] how blind we are to the fatal consequence of living aloof from the spirit of love. Surely each one of us in his heart must humbly acknowledge shortcomings too plain to be denied. Surely we must confess it a shame and a scandal that, with ideals so sublime before our eyes, we are so little consecrated to the holy purposes of Christian love, so selfish and inconsiderate and unsympathetic and hard, and even hateful.

Is it not true? Study the life of the average Catholic; take note of the daily conduct of ordinary men and women like you and me. What evidence is there in our lives to show that we have heartily accepted the gospel of love preached by Jesus Christ, that our existence is controlled by the one supreme purpose of growing in love of God and love of our fellowmen? Note our daily routine, our employment of time, our expenditure of money, our tone of speech, the trend of our desires and efforts, the spirit even of our prayers and petitions. Think how we behave when we are overworked, disappointed,

[24] John 15:12.

41

irritated, passionate, humiliated, or threatened with some calamity.

In our lives, who can discover the hourly evidence of an overmastering desire to postpone all other things to the cultivation of a deeper love for God and our neighbor? Yet this it is that our hearts would be really set upon, were the words and example of Jesus Christ the model of our daily behavior. We are born brethren of those early Christians who took so literally the admonition of the aged apostle: "Little children, love one another." We are far-off followers of those who lived out the characteristics described by Paul in his wonderful painting of love: patient, kind, unenvying, unsuspicious, without pride or perversity, tirelessly enduring all things, and never falling away.[25]

It all suggests that perhaps we are misapplying much effort. Our strivings for salvation have to be redirected. We should pray and labor to become more unselfish, more loving. We must get into the habit of thinking less of ourselves and our own interests. We must acquire the point of view that will enable us to realize that our one

[25] 1 Cor. 13:4-7.

chance of being admitted to Christ's kingdom lies in our absorbing some of that spirit of self-sacrificing love that drew Him down from Heaven to give Himself up entirely for the sake of His Father and His brethren. The same Father and the same brethren are ours. And the thing above all other things to be heartily desired is that, for love of that Father and those brethren, we shall unselfishly live and unselfishly die.

Chapter Four

God Desires
Union with You

✣

The Christ Child attracts the hearts of all
The Christ Child! What magic in the name! As if awak-
ened by an angel's singing, we behold the vision: a great
host gathered beneath the midnight stars, straining with
eyes and hands toward a radiant figure, symbol of all
human hopes, all human fears — a newborn Child.
Kneeling beside Him, Mary, maid and mother, Joseph,
husband and father, the shepherds and the kings adore.

Familiar faces we see, out of every tribe, tongue, people, and nation. Jewish fishermen stand beside Athenian
philosophers, Praetorian guardsmen, and Nubian slaves.
Parthians and Medes and Elamites and inhabitants of Mes-
opotamia are there,[26] young and aged, vigorous and crip-
pled, the beggar and the king. Celts and Saxons press
forward in the throng, swineherds, monks, serfs, plowmen,
jesters; Huns and Goths and Danes, penitent warriors

[26] Cf. Acts 2:9.

and Vikings, converted pirates and freebooters. Children of a later growth, too, have come: bishops, knights, artists, scholars, troubadours, merchants, and craftsmen from medieval Umbria and Provence and Castile and Normandy, from the Rhine and Yorkshire and Armagh. And strange pilgrims bring the tribute of the newer world: conquistadores, black-robed missionaries, friars in white and brown and gray, with their neophytes, Mohawks, Chinese, Eskimos, Filipinos — all crowding the vast spaces to gaze upon the heavenly Infant with adoring eyes.

The vision fades. And then the mind travels back, to that distant day in the infancy of the human race when God first promised a Redeemer to our fallen parents, the day when man went out from Paradise, his heart already kindling with a hope never to be extinguished through centuries as dark as paganism could make them. Far and wide his wanderings led, yet, no matter to what low, brutish level his soul might sink, ever the promise hung star-like above his unsteady course; ever, benignly shining in the darkness, it saved him from utter despair. The broad world over, amid dull savages in arctic ice-huts, among faraway, fierce tribes of the south, on trackless mountain ranges and on scorched plains alike — everywhere, man, living upon the dim memory of a divine assurance, dwelt in the hope of a Savior to come.

To God's chosen people, that promise became the foundation of a national faith, the inspiring motive of a heroic struggle against every temptation to abandon hope. Throughout all the varied history of the Jews, it shone steady, in the rainbow's splendid colors, in evening cloud, in sunset star. God had pledged His word, and the midnight horizon of life was finally to be burnished with the glow of dawn. Ever and again by word of seer or saint, the promise bursts out prophetically; by victory and by miracle, it is confirmed. The dream of a God to come! A charm so potent against the demon of despair! A vision that illumines the darkest human experience!

Christ comes into your life quietly

Behold here the fulfillment — as simple as the tale told by a child, as commonplace as any incident of the passing day. Not with whirlwind, nor with earthquake, nor in fire, but as the breathing of a gentle air was the coming of the Lord[27] — quiet, modest, unimpressive, as

[27] 3 Kings 19:11-13 (RSV = 1 Kings 19:11-13).

the delicate shading of an autumn sunrise noted only by the artist's vigilant senses, as the faint echoing of far-off chimes, which only a listening ear detects.

Thus, almost in secret, came the Son of God to earth. The simplicity of it overwhelms us. It is marvelous that the Creator of Heaven and earth should come to be made man; it is all but incredible that He, the Infinite One, should come so humbly.

Divest the scene of the significance attached by faith. Contemplate it with the eyes of sense alone. Take into account only what is visible and palpable. Nothing will then capture the imagination, nothing startle the emotions. And, indeed, we see from the behavior of the people of the time that the great event of human history passed almost entirely unnoticed. Poet and consul and emperor, too occupied with their own affairs even to heed the report of it, went on their way. They received Him not; yet the Christ Child was their God.

Such was His way of acting in that day. Such is His way at the present time as well. Even at this moment, we may be looking at some wonderful divine event, without recognizing its significance. We may daily be trifling with sublime privileges and wasting God-given opportunities.

The thought suggests a pointed question: Are we really blind to the deep significance of the Christ Child? Are we content with a conventional notion of what Christmas means? Amid the holly and the green, do our hearts expand with merely human sentiment? Do we impart and receive a joy that is all of the earth, earthly?

If so, then to us, Christian and Catholic though we be, this blessed birth may bring no increase of faith, no deepening of trust, no new growth of love in the service of God. Then we, like the Pharisees, so hard of heart, may look on the God of love and know Him not. Frivolous and unaware, we prattle about our petty interests.

We, unto whom is born a Savior who is Christ the Lord, the Wonderful One, the Counselor, the Mighty God, the Prince of Peace[28] — could we but realize all that His coming really implies, we might thereby gain everything that is needed to perfect our unsatisfactory lives, to make us fit for close and loving association with God, to render us truly religious.

[28] Luke 2:11; Isa. 9:6.

Be of Good Heart

God created you to be united with Him

What is religion? Turning aside from the thought of
forms and creed, ceasing for the moment to advert to the
Church, her sacraments, her laws, and her varied life of
devotion, consider what underlies these visible appearances. They are indeed divine means for the obtaining
of a divine end; but behind them, an inspiring cause, primary, essential, springing out of the very constitution of
humanity and the nature of God, is something that may
be regarded as at once the justification and the end of all
religion: the vocation of the human soul to enter into
loving union with its Maker.

That my soul might finally be united to Him is the end
God had in view in creating me, in redeeming me, and
in accomplishing each one of a long series of miracles of
grace that He has wrought. My life is utterly useless, my
soul will perish hopelessly, if that end be missed. Every
moment of my existence, every thought and word and act
of mine, is to be assayed according to the standard of that
divine purpose. Whatever makes for union with God is
good, noble, and holy; whatever lessens union is vain,
base, and wicked. The chance of being united with Him,

and that alone, explains the true reason of my existence and of the existence of every man created.

The supreme aim of religion, then, is to consummate the union of the soul with God. Religion that does not promise it is an absurdity; religion that does not help to achieve it is a sham.

But dare any religion give us hope of what is so inconceivably beyond both our merit and our power? We men and women, so unimportant, so unlovely — are we sought in love by the almighty Being who dug out the sea and hung the stars and shaped the course of heaven's flying meteors? Is it credible that He desires to unite us with Himself in a union more intimate than any ever realized by human lovers? The thought is overwhelming. Why, many a *mortal* is so gifted, so famous, or so powerful that we dare not aspire to *his* friendship! Shall we then hope for companionship and loving union with the omnipotent God? Surely He is too great; surely we are too little.

And if ever God seemed oppressively great, in this age more than in any other does He seem so. Of old, people cherished notions that made of God a sort of larger man. With fancies as simple as the thoughts of children, with a background painted only half-consciously by the imagination, they pictured Him in the likeness of themselves and appreciated merely the smallest part of His power.

A small stretch of land was then the universe; heaven was swung overhead almost within reach; sun and stars were gaps through which celestial light was shining. The God who walked in the cool of the evening,[29] the God whose messenger could hardly overcome the wrestling Jacob[30] — He, indeed, might confidently be approached.

But today our knowledge of the extent of His creation awes us. God's image grows greater with every step of advancing science. As the ocean's depths are sounded, wonder is added to wonder. Plant and animal and man daily reveal new miracles, new mysteries. We look into the distant sky, we measure from star to star, and we are overwhelmed by an endless vista in a universe that is infinite. In short, the divine majesty has become something that we can prove, that we can see and feel, that strikes home, that weighs upon us and crushes us down with a sense of our own littleness. We know now the greatness of the

[29] Cf. Gen. 3:8.
[30] Gen. 32:24-28.

chasm to be bridged before man can look upon the face of God. The noonday of human science blazes out splendidly, but as we look upward, our eyes are stricken blind.

What has religion now to say? Must it not be silent? Blessed, indeed, were the ancients in their childlike faith. We admire their simplicity, and we envy them their boldness of affection. But we who have been made aware of God's real greatness, on whom there has been impressed so terrifying a sense of His power, dare not presume to call Him friend. We are struck with wonder; we praise the immensity and the harmony of His work; we cry out proudly with the psalmist, "Who is a God like unto our God?"[31] But we do not venture to add, "The God of no other nation is so near to them as our God is near to us."[32] Our inheritance of knowledge oppresses us, and our sense of the divine magnificence strikes us dumb. Hope is chilled in the heart. We shall admire God, but none of us shall venture to call Him friend.

Then comes ringing the angel's message: "This day is born to you a Savior who is Christ the Lord."[33] We turn

[31] Ps. 76:14 (RSV = Ps. 77:13).
[32] Cf. Deut. 4:7.
[33] Luke 2:11.

to the crib of Bethlehem, and there we behold our God in swaddling clothes! He, the Everlasting, the Omnipotent, the Infinite, has become, for love's sake, a creature, a human being, the Christ Child on His maiden Mother's breast.

No word is needed. We look; we realize. Now life is all changed for us. Henceforth, nothing is impossible. There is nothing we may not hope for, since this is true. We can think of no height too high for human aspiration, no depth too low for God to meet us there. Young man and maiden, father and mother, child and elder, we kneel beside the Christmas Crib, each confident of welcome. Emmanuel! God with us:[34] He is not too good, nor too great; He is our Friend and Brother. He has come to abide — yes, to abide always. Through storm of temptation and stress of weakness and weight of sin pressed down upon us, He will be with us still — Jesus, the Christ Child, yesterday and today and the same forever.[35]

[34] Matt. 1:23.
[35] Cf. Heb. 13:8.

Chapter Five
❧

Your Soul Can Be Renewed

Through Christ, you have become a child of God
The greatest event of all human history was the moment when, "in the fullness of time, God sent His Son, made of a woman, that we might become adopted sons."[36]

Ponder the richness of meaning contained in those words: "God sent His Son." Jesus Christ, Mary's Babe, is as truly God as is the eternal Father. He is a revelation of divinity, God made manifest in the flesh, in order that all who look upon Him may begin to understand God's beauty and goodness and sanctity. This Holy One is God's Son by right, and He has come to make it possible for us sinners to become sons of God by adoption, so that, in some true way, we may resemble Him and acquire those qualities which belong to God alone.

Recall for a moment what the Church teaches: that Christ's grace restores us, although with certain

[36] Gal. 4:4.

restrictions, to that original state of holiness which belonged to man before the Fall. Included in that original endowment had been the gift of divine sonship. Man had been adopted as one of God's own kindred; he had been united to God by wonderful bonds of sympathy and understanding and love; he had received the gift of the Holy Spirit and had been allowed to share in qualities that were divine. To man thus constituted in a life of happiness and holiness, temptation presented itself; and he, selfishly seeking his own apparent advantage, deliberately forsook the life of love. In so doing, he lost God; he fell from the position to which he had been elevated.

Shorn of grace, man sank to the lower level of earth, henceforth excluded from the privileged intimacy that had once been his, unable even to commune with God. Shut out of Paradise, capable only of blind, ineffectual gropings after the beauty and the truth and the goodness possessed in happier days, he was doomed to endless misery, had not God come to save him. As we know, God did come. Jesus was born here upon earth, so that man might receive again the adoption of sonship, might again be admitted to divine life and friendship. The human soul is thus again enabled to converse intimately with its Maker, knowing and loving Him and in turn being loved by Him in a fashion and degree natural not even to the angels.

Such is the Catholic doctrine concerning the Fall of man and his subsequent restoration. It is a brief statement of the most critical period in the history of the human race. It is something more personal than this as well, for it suggests to our individual memories great critical moments in our own past experience.

That which happened to mankind has happened also to us individually. We, too, are looking back through shadowy years to a distant day of innocence and holiness, when all was well with us and we lived very near to God. We, too, remember days passed in the light and glory of the divine presence, when prayer was easy and obedience willing and temptation not hard to overcome.

Far distant days, indeed, they seem to us now. We look back to them as some patriarch may have looked back to the golden age of Paradise, as a banished man looks back to his home country and his childhood, with inexpressible yearning to turn back the flight of time.

If only once again, as in happier years, I might look up into the face of God, reverent, yet unafraid! If ten or twenty or fifty years of life could be blotted out, and I could again be the child I was that day long ago, before I ever stumbled into evil paths and turned my back upon God, who made me!

Is it a wild hope, an impossible dream? Does the past remain utterly irrevocable? Can sin never be undone? Or is there still a chance that some mighty intervention of the omnipotent hand of God may even now roll away the years, efface the consequences of our criminal disobedience, and restore to us again the holiness and the joy that were ours in that ancient day when, yet unstained by sin, we really were the children of God? Is it possible to be born again?

Christ makes your soul new

Jesus Christ, in the crib at Bethlehem, is our answer. He, the infinite God, begotten of the Father before all ages, has come to be born again in time, in order that the whole race of man may be reborn, in order that you and I and every wicked sinner may become what He is here: a little child.

This answer staggers the mind. It would seem too hard to believe, if we did not see Him here. Even after looking upon Him, we would imagine we had mistaken the significance of His coming, were it not that the Holy Spirit tells us plainly what it means: "God sent His Son . . . that we might become adopted sons."

We may take heart, then, those of us who sigh for the return of a day long past and for the restoration of our vanished virtue. It is precisely for the accomplishment of such a miracle that Jesus Christ has come. We have but to sink down on penitent knees before our Brother who is born for us and ask for the grace to be born again for Him. Just as surely as we ask with sincerity, the request will be granted to us.

We shall be made children again.

What then?

Of course, we shall be children who resemble our Brother. Of course, we shall abide with Him, look constantly upon Him, heed His every word, and copy in our feeble way His every deed.

Living thus in His likeness, we shall always remain children in the wonderful sense in which He Himself never ceases to remain a child.

Be of Good Heart

Years that force the body to mature and to decay
and die will work no alteration of our spirit; in time and
eternity, we shall be like this Child, our elder Brother,
the firstborn of all His many brethren.[37] Years that fail to
rob us of our innocence will be equally unable to deprive
us of our joy. The simple delight that fills the unspoiled
heart of the child, the peace that is the characteristic
spirit of Christmas and in some little measure is shared
by the poorest and the worst at such a season — this will
become our permanent possession when once we have
put on the spirit of the Christ of Bethlehem.

Each day, we open a new chapter of our lives. Many
a secret the future withholds from us; many a surprise it
keeps in store. Still we can forecast much. Clearly enough
we see, even now, burdens we shall have to endure, temptations we must encounter, a summons we shall surely
receive to unselfish sacrifice and heroic endeavor. Even
now we know, as well as we shall ever know, upon what
the issue will depend; we know what we must do to be
both happy and holy, just as, on the other hand, we
know well the course of conduct that brings ruin.

[37] Rom. 8:29.

God's glory must be the motive of all you do

"Glory to God!"[38] This is the first and foremost aim of Jesus Christ. "At the beginning of the book, it is written of me: Behold I come to do Thy will, O God."[39] Thus did our Lord Himself express His sense of the primary motive of His coming.

So, too, at the beginning of the book of every good life, and at the head of every chapter, must be written, "Glory to God!" So, too, before starting out upon any undertaking, we must remind ourselves that God's glory, not our own selfish interest, is to be the guiding principle and the dominant motive of all our activity.

"Glory to God!" It rings out in the refrain of the angelic choirs passing and repassing over the head of the newborn Babe as He lies in His manger at Bethlehem. It keeps echoing in our ears after we have gone away out into the world again. And it must resound within our souls over and over, always and ever, in the crises of great temptation, in sore moments of disappointment, under

[38] Luke 2:14.
[39] Cf. Ps. 39:8-9 (RSV = Ps. 40:7-8).

the stress of tormenting pain. So shall our weakness be stayed up, in the hour of need, by the familiar music of those heavenly words: "Glory to God!"

"And peace to men."[40] It was by bringing peace upon earth that Christ gave glory to God. In the same way shall we fulfill our divinely appointed destiny. May that destiny be enthusiastically realized. May our coming and our going, our speaking and our doing, ever further the growth of that peace which is the condition of human happiness. May we renounce our pleasures, surrender our plans, and sacrifice our hopes, readily and gladly, whenever by so doing we shall add to the sum of human joy and bring peace upon earth to men of good will.

"Glory to God and peace to men": it is our motto for life, because it is the motto of our Brother, and it is to be worn by every adopted son of God.

---

[40] Luke 2:14.

Chapter Six

⊰

You Can Be Assured of Christ's Love for You

✢

Christ's Passion proves His love for you
Even more than to liberty, we may say to love: "What crimes are committed in thy name!"[41] Yet, although base passions daily masquerade as love, although its sacred name is taken in vain, blasphemed, and worn as a cloak for sin, it still retains its power to charm. Not even the hatred of hatred stirs men so effectually as the love of love.

Contrasted with all other manifestations of love, the life of Jesus Christ is unique, supreme, resembling no other thing except the answering love it has itself inspired in the hearts of men. Two great truths are clear to those who have looked on Christ: that, in love, He was more than man, and that, imitating Him, we can be more than human. Love was the measure of His greatness; it must be ours.

[41] Marie-Jeanne Roland: "O liberty! O liberty! What crimes are committed in thy name!" in A. de Lamartine, *Histoire des Girondins*, Bk. 51, ch. 8.

Saints seem to have learned the nature of Christ's love best by the study of His Passion. Indeed, no soul that has meditated on that supreme tragedy can ever totally forget it. One who has contemplated Christ dying is apt to go about as a man who has heard his own death sentence spoken.

Jesus, the kindest, the best, the strongest, and the tenderest of friends, our support in toil, our comrade in temptation and suffering, bowed His head in death upon the Cross after hours of indescribable anguish. Thinking of this, we remember also the bottomless depths of depression into which His soul was swept during the frightful Agony in the Garden, when the dread forebodings of the future wrung blood from every pore in His quivering body.[42] Even now, centuries after the event, those vivid scenes come before us and are branded on our imaginations painfully, indelibly.

Yet, for all its horror, the Passion is the seal and stamp of a heavenly consolation. Christ's agony forestalled, prevented ours. By His stripes have we been healed.[43] We do

[42] Luke 22:43-44.
[43] 1 Pet. 2:24.

not contemplate the dying figure on the Cross without being reminded of our own redemption through the Pre· cious Blood then poured forth in such abundance. The atonement wrought by Christ has, we remember, saved us from inevitable and eternal misery, has brought us our divine opportunity, our one chance of Heaven. Ill should we have fared had not He suffered, for, even now, rescued from the abyss and set upon the road to Paradise, we find the achievement of our salvation still a task of enormous difficulty.

Behind our sense of suffering, then, lies a sense of gratitude. We shrink at the thought of Christ's Passion, and yet we are thankful that He went through those dark and bloody ways, treading His lonely path of anguish, so that the multitude of men might be spared the final anguish of separation from God. In those moments, He was bearing on His own shoulders the burden He knew would be too heavy for our strength, and amid the all-but-unrelieved blackness of Passiontide grief shines this one golden ray.

We look back at the horror of what then was done, but also we look forward to the great things that it is now possible for us to do — for the crime of Christ's murderers may be in some sense expiated by our repentance. The sorrows that once encompassed Him are to be swallowed up in His greater joy, when the salvation of His sinful brethren is assured. This thought comes like a new inspiration, an impelling conviction. We must go forward where He has led; we must follow Him and, if necessary, die with Him. By showing for us a love such as no other has ever shown, He summons and persuades us to love Him in like manner.

Christ Himself appealed to His Passion as a test of His love for man. Weighed thus, His love stands out as the unique love of human history. Never before had men been loved, never again could men be loved, as deeply as Christ Jesus loved them. For love is tested in the crucible of suffering; and no human heart ever passed through so fiery a torment as that to which our Savior was subjected. The love that survived that test ranks first, forever.

We are well aware of the common course of human love. It thrives upon joy; it is eager for pleasure and satisfaction; it is chilled and numbed by disappointment; it crumbles under the repeated blows of pain. Naturally, men begin to love what pleases; naturally, too, they love no longer when love becomes a source of suffering. A month, a year, a stretch of years one's love may last, when conditions are all favorable. But repelled, scorned, and lashed with the whips of ingratitude, selfishness, and pain, human love does not endure.

Jesus Christ, however, loved with a love more intense than the pain by which He was tortured. He loved us while He foresaw the coming of this pain; He loved us amid the worst throes of His Passion; and His love outlasted the blasphemous rejoicings of His triumphant executioners. Bethlehem finds upon Calvary the perfect fulfillment of its promise of love. The uttermost word possible to God or to man, in the way of love, is spoken in Gethsemane, along the Via Dolorosa, from the Cross of Golgotha.

Christ's Passion awakens heroic love

The records of Christian sanctity show how wonderful a response the Passion has evoked from human hearts down through the centuries, in every corner of the earth, and in every walk of life. In always-widening circles, around that rough and bloodstained tree converted into a throne, the purest and the strongest among our race's children have gathered by unnumbered thousands, each new generation sending a new host of lovers thrilled, captivated by the spell of the Cross.

What was not possible to mere nature has actually been realized through the marvelous power of redeeming grace. Weak flesh and blood have given birth to men and women heroic enough to open up new worlds of possibility for the human soul. There is nothing conceivable that the lovers of the Cross of Christ have not been able to achieve. The promises of this world of low desire, the threats uttered by bodily and spiritual foes, the apparent darkening of God's countenance — all these have been made light of, unselfishly braved, by hearts grown super-human through the consciousness of Christian love. That story of love is the fairest chapter in all human history. And, but for the Passion, it would never have been written at all.

Passiontide brings all this home to us with the force of a direct appeal. It is with deep purpose that the Church persuades us yearly to gather together and to meditate upon the story of our Savior's agony. She would have us become so impenetrated with the sense of His great love for us and of our possibility of great love for Him, that into our lives there may come a change transforming us — even us — into holy men and women, capable of loving God with the heroic love of saints.

Some change, some improvement, all of us surely need. Our best has never yet been realized. Each year, there is the new chance that the perfect chapter of our lives may now begin. From sin to repentance, perhaps; from indifference to affection; from lukewarm service to the enthusiasm of devotedness; from commonplace selfishness to holy love — these are the alterations that may be wrought in us according to our needs and our generous purpose.

Few will hesitate to admit that, up to this moment, their lives have not been sufficiently fruitful: few will be content to go before the judgment seat with no more to their credit than what they have earned thus far; few are unaware of evil habits, more or less serious, not yet wholly eradicated; few feel free of unsatisfied aspirations and disappointed spiritual ambitions.

By one and all, of whatever moral stature, let the same great truth be pondered: love is the beginning of religion and its end. Divine love expressed itself in the Passion of Christ with a fullness above the power of the human mind to measure; and the memory of the redeeming Blood poured forth during that Passion has made men and women supernatural in the strength of their love of God. There is no sinner in all the wide world who may not, by the grace of that same Precious Blood, if he so wills, be converted into a saint.

What are the common obstacles to improvement? Are they not, generally speaking, pleasant things we will not renounce, or unpleasant things we refuse to do? Be we beginners or far advanced on the road to holiness, it is ever the same. The issue lies always between distasteful duty and pleasant sin, between God and self, between love and indulgence.

Christ's Passion teaches you how to love Him

Perhaps the stirring spell of the Passion of Christ, its ability to sway and move, and its magic power to make weak men into heroes, is due to the fact that, when we look upon the face of the dying Christ and number His wounds and watch His dripping Blood, we necessarily lose something of our fear of pain, something of our devotion to personal comfort and sensuous delight. That is the reason the great spiritual teacher of the world, Holy Church, prudent mother and wise guide, never lets the eyes of her children wander far away from the vision of the Cross.

That is the reason — insofar as human reason is capable of discerning the reason — why the story of the great masters of divine love is always the story of a man or a woman contemplating a crucifix.

The Cross of Jesus Christ tells us of the possibilities within ourselves. Look on the Man of Sorrows,[44] and say what it is He bids us do. Is it not, in one word, to love Him despite every obstacle and every discouragement? It is as if, dying upon the Cross, He had called out to us for aid. And go to Him we must through fire and flood; go to Him we will, even though it cost comfort and riches and friends and health and life itself. For He has spilled out His last drop of Blood for our salvation, and we should deserve the lowest hell were we callous to the appeal of His dying lips. One who has suffered thus for us shall not call on us in vain.

That is the message of Passiontide. The bleeding figure who hangs upon Calvary's Cross is the Friend and Savior of our souls. He has laid down His life for love of us; He has laid down His life to show us how to love Him in return.

[44] Isa. 53:3.

Chapter Seven

⁂

There Is a Perfect Life to Come

Learn to see beyond this life

Carpe Diem![45] Seize the day as it flies! Eat, drink, and be merry. Meet not the tragic fate of the man who saves up for a future he is never to behold!

This is the world's philosophy, based on human instinct not controlled. See it revealed in the child with his shining toy, unconscious for the moment of any interest but his play. See it in the young man aglow with the rapture of his first success. See it in the radiant girl, treading the rose-strewn paths of maiden love. See it in every man with his riches and his friendship and his kindred. All alike are content with the present and careless of the future; they think they already grasp the elements of perfect joy; they forget the unseen, the unattained.

But if we thus neglect the ideal, and dwell instead upon the fullness and richness of our present possessions;

[45] Horace, *Odes*, Bk. 1, no. 11, line 7.

if the spirit grows blind in proportion as we become
familiar with the glory and the treasures of the physical
world; if we liken ourselves to the plants that grow and
the beasts that breed, without restraint for the present
or concern for the future — then, indeed, we have sore
need of some divine influence that shall lift us up out
of the mire of this spiritual desolation and set us upon
a height whence we may behold again the littleness of
earth and the measureless expanse of Heaven.

Humanly speaking, it is only when the hair is white,
when age has come and life is almost over, that men
begin to realize how hopelessly elusive is the happiness
promised by wealth and fame and love and power; how
vain are the pursuits in which youth and freshness have
been wasted; how truly the real value of life lies in its
opportunities for the accomplishment of invisible, ideal,
eternally enduring results.

It is to forestall the bitter experiences of a wasted life
and to induce men in good time to direct their efforts
toward the proper end, that Christ became our teacher.

Of all lessons, is it not the inadequacy of the present
that we find it hardest to learn? What is the matter
with us, but that we are petty and short-sighted and

small-minded, that we fail to view things with eternal
eyes? If we are ever to realize our great destiny, we must
learn to appreciate the insignificance of the present
except as the symbol and vehicle of the future; we must
know that the supreme end of our endeavor is in this
life unattainable.

Think of those old tormenting questions: Why did
Christ appear to another generation and not to ours?
Why did He burst the shackles of death and rise from
the tomb, if He was not to bless the earth forever with
His presence? Indeed, why should He ever have assumed
a body of flesh at all, unless in obedience to an irresistible
desire to live with men, unless He wished always to be
uplifting humanity by the inspiration of His word and
His example?

We ask why, but the answer is clear. Christ came in
human form chiefly for the purpose of awakening man
to a sense of divine possibilities. He rose visibly from the
dead in order to bear witness to the truth of His message.
He vanished into the unseen world again to emphasize
the fact that the battle is still unwon and human perfection still unattained, to show that only in the life beyond
do we arrive at the real goal of our existence.

Be of Good Heart

Belief in Christ implies a facing toward the future, a confession of the inadequacy of the present. Only in another state of existence and at a distant time will the reward of the disciple be given, and the wage of the laborer be paid; there and then only shall the weary be at rest, and the soldier be free to lay down his arms. The immediate purpose of Christ's earthly existence was fulfilled when once He had flashed the vision of a perfect life before humanity's wondering eyes. Forever after, His figure and His story would be sure to break in upon the dreams of a slumbering world and trouble its self-contentment. The risen Christ could never be wholly forgotten. So long as that lesson haunted human memory, the present, the visible, the merely natural could never suffice to quench the thirst in the soul of man.

Christ, then, willed to bestow upon us a new conception of life, to erect a new scale of values. He gave to men's eyes a fresh perception of spiritual beauty. He stirred men's souls with a new discontent. He made it forever impossible that His disciples should be satisfied with the things produced by earth. Into their hearts He flung the dart of a divine ambition; before their sight He flashed the image of Godlike possibilities. To the meanest of human creatures was granted the opportunity of one day sharing in the life of God.

The risen Christ strengthens and consoles you

Man was spurred on by the promise. His way was lighted by the heavenly vision. And on it all, Christ's Resurrection set the seal of infallible security. Like the desire of the moth for the star, of the day for the morrow, that hope burns quenchlessly in human breasts, as men and women toil slowly up the heights of more-than-human sanctity. If they faint not, it is because they know that Christ, risen from the dead, goes before them.

Sometimes doubt afflicts a man. Then the vision of the risen Christ appears. It is as if a whisper from Heaven had been uttered and the voice of God had commanded us to put away hesitation, to cast out fear, and to trust in the goodness of the Father, who sent us Christ and who promises to give Him to us again forever.

Sometimes a man is tempted. Then the risen Christ speaks to us of victory through renunciation and of salvation through the Cross. The deceits of sin are exposed in all their miserable trickery; the curtain is raised for our eyes to behold the joys of Heaven; and Jesus is seen again, as

Be of Good Heart

Stephen saw Him, at the right hand of the Father,[46] looking down with smiling lips and loving gesture, inviting us to follow. What assurance it gives a man when, in the stress of conflict, he thus feels Christ urging and God aiding him! What strength comes then to the arm, what hope to the heart!

Sometimes a man is stricken with sorrow. It may be that an unforeseen calamity has fallen upon him and that life is blighted. He is reduced from comfort to poverty. Bodily ills (or mental torment) make existence almost insupportable. Or the cruel hand of death has torn a dear one from him, with possibly the added anguish that he was far away and only strangers' eyes could watch and only alien hands could serve the one he loved so tenderly. If so, how much it means to him to see beyond the clouds a fairer life unmarred by sin or sorrow, to believe that our Savior's smile is gladdening the heart he was so helpless to console, to know that the day will come when to him also He will open the gate of the everlasting Paradise.

And sometimes a man is hungry and thirsty for the things of the soul; he is afire with the ambition of

---

[46] Acts 7:55 (RSV = Acts 7:56).

righteousness; his heart is set on holiness. When sin sickens us and sanctity attracts, how precious is the ideal embodied in the scene of Easter morn: Christ rising from the grave, His message of pardon and hope now justified eternally, His promise vindicated forevermore!

Thus, then, has the risen Christ shaped and perfected human life, assuaging our griefs, overcoming our difficulties, deepening our sense of sin, and strengthening our longing for holiness; for to everyone who follows Him, He promises a good infinitely above all that the mind of itself could conceive or the heart desire.[47]

Christ's Resurrection enlightens the whole world
And the Resurrection has affected not only the individual, but also the world. At this distance of time, it is hard for us to realize how greatly the social order was changed by the leaven of that inspiration. Yet even a superficial acquaintance with the best men and the noblest institutions of paganism lets us see that the pre-Christian age was the day of the omnipotent present. Men lived for visible goods. Bread and the public games, war and the

---

[47] Cf. 1 Cor. 2:9.

power it brought — these were the things looming largest in the general consciousness. In politics, in art, in ethics, and in religion, the existing generation and the visible horizon bounded man's best and highest interests. The welfare of the state was an ultimate end; and by relation to it was every right justified and every duty prescribed. The philosophers Plato and Aristotle, Seneca, Epictetus and Marcus Aurelius — these were indeed noble; but we find vital defects in their conduct and fatal inconsistency in their principles.

Looking back, we may be disposed to see things glorified through the mist of centuries, and tinged with the glamour of bygone days. There is old Rome at the head of the world with its ideal of universal military conquest practically realized; and we cannot but feel a sense of enthusiasm and exaltation as we note the flashing eagles and catch the glint of sun-tipped lances, as we hear the tramp of legionaries and measure the majestic sweep of Roman law. But we forget the wailing of the abandoned infant, the shame of the unblushing woman, and the unspeakable degradation of the slave.

There is Greece for the eye to rest upon, a star in the night, a pinnacle rising out of the silent ocean of antiquity, the fair home of philosophy and the temple of art. But Greece's sages treat of the breeding of men as of so many cattle, and discuss forms of aesthetic expression that must remain forever nameless in an age of Christian enlightenment.

One need not attempt to show that, in the matter of personal virtue, an individual Christian is always the superior of a pagan; but let the two systems be set in contrast. In the Roman amphitheater, they confront each other — here, on the benches, the intoxicated crowd, delirious, absorbed, fascinated with the present, shouting their savage joy, and with down-turned thumbs demanding the blood of victims; there, on the crimson sands, the little group of martyrs serenely facing the future.

Into this dark age of the ascendant present steals Christianity like the glow of dawn. Around time is thrown the luminous halo of eternity. Out of the human soul are evoked unsuspected possibilities. Slowly, as figures that take shape in the soft, gray morning, new principles and institutions begin to outline themselves. Sublime teachings strike root and blossom in the hearts of men. For the first time, the absolute sanctity of human life is impressed on the public consciousness. A strange new doctrine about the dignity of labor and the glory of serving is revealed. Hereafter, in the sight of God, there can be no distinction of persons. A mystical word is spoken, and forth from the darkness starts a gracious vision of beauty, the Christian woman, to hover above the race in its progress onward, to be the symbol of all things lovely and sacred, to set the halo of chastity on the brow of the mother of men.

Then begins that long procession of saints, the like of which history never knew before: Paul, Sebastian (the soldier), Augustine (philosopher and penitent), Agnes, Cecilia, Catherine, Teresa, Joan, Francis, Philip, Vincent, and Damien. All the old nobility of nature remains; and added to it, gracing it, come new qualities, strange, striking, and divine — the fruit of that seed which the gospel had sown in the world.

A new influence is at work; man's sleep is disturbed; the luminous figure of the risen Christ is haunting his dreams. Caught in the spell of an ideal not of earth, life is wonderfully transformed; for, as surely as the daylight comes from this sun shining over our heads, so surely have the blessings of our civilization come from belief in the risen Christ and from response to Christian inspiration.

So, if the soul is greater than the body and truth fairer than a lie; if it is nobler to die a martyr than to live a traitor and a coward; if to love faithfully is better than to lust; if to render justice to the meanest serf is manlier than to slay a helpless enemy — then it is Christ we must thank for those ideals which are highest, and for those achievements which are worthiest to be recorded.

Easter reminds us of this; it tells us, in a way, why it was expedient that Christ should go; it shows us what the sending of His Spirit has done for the individual and for the world.[48] It bids us remember that we have not here a lasting city,[49] but are pilgrims making our journey slowly and with difficulty toward a country that is afar. There has Christ gone before us; there He has prepared a place for us; there He Himself awaits us — He, Christ, the Lord, who was slain but is alive; who was buried, but is risen. Alleluia!

[48] John 16:7.
[49] Heb. 13:14.

Chapter Eight

Do Not Let Suffering Discourage You

Christ prepares you for troubles

About to ascend into Heaven, our Lord speaks to the
disciples, to prepare them for His going. A new epoch
is now to begin. Men and women hitherto supported by
the visible presence of the Savior are henceforth to walk
alone — looking forward indeed to the day that will
reunite disciple and Master, but meanwhile journeying
through the darkness of lifelong separation. It is a moment
inexpressibly solemn, a moment full of sadness.

Our Lord's words are little calculated to lessen the
apprehension of the disciples. What He says is far from
reassuring to flesh and blood. He foretells a time of
persecution and suffering. The disciples are to experience
a great testing of faith: they will be expelled from the
synagogue; they will be hunted down like wild beasts;
they will be destroyed as enemies of God.[50] Insult,

---

[50] Cf. John 16:2.

banishment, suffering, death — such is His bequest to them. Enthroned in glory at the right hand of the Father, He will look down and see His followers writhing in the flames and on the rack; He will hear them invoke His Name as they are tortured and done to death. And He will not intervene.

Nothing could be clearer, then, than Christ's intention to promise His disciples no freedom from suffering, no protection against bodily pain. He gives them no assurance of temporal reward. Calmly, as if outlining His own plan, He promises them persecution. This, then, is something that fits perfectly into His design. And when it comes, there will be no excuse for panic or apprehension.

What was it He had said? "Remember that I told you."[51] It will be necessary only to recall His word, and to be faithful to the ever-present grace of the Spirit. On this one condition, all will come to a happy ending; and the heavier burden of suffering will be but the measure of the greater final joy.

How quickly and how accurately our Savior's prediction was verified. Turn over the pages of the Acts of the

[51] John 16:4.

Apostles. Hardly had the Holy Spirit come when the era of persecution dawned. Generation after generation witnessed the attempt to drown the Christian Faith in the blood of martyrs. Rack and scourge, sword and fire, burning at the stake and crucifixion — every means that diabolical ingenuity could devise was used against Christ's followers. Yet all in vain! Strong in the strength of the Spirit sent by their Master, weak men, frail women, and little children were able to defy the fury of the world and the malice of the powers of darkness. Not delivered from suffering, they were able to overcome it.

Pain, ceasing to be the ruler of the human soul, became a guide to new and splendid heights of glory. For this is the victory achieved by the divine Spirit coming down into the dark places of the world and visiting the timid and the weak. He illumines them with heavenly light and lifts them forever beyond the influence of cowardly fear. The saint dreads nothing, for nothing can conquer his soul.

The Holy Spirit strengthens you

To us also the Paraclete was promised, and in our lives, too, the prediction made by Jesus has been verified. The advent of the Spirit has been followed by times of trial and often by great suffering. Is it not consoling to be assured that such affliction is not a sign of God's displeasure, nor an indication that our Savior has abandoned us, but rather a necessary condition of progress toward the state of holiness that is our destiny?

After all, the lesson we most need to learn is that which teaches us how to bear trials and endure suffering. Inevitably nature will protest against what is unpleasant; nature will argue; nature will rebel. How many good people, even apparently spiritual people, complain when trial comes — almost as if they thought our Lord had promised that no disciple of His should ever have to bear a cross! How many times temporal prosperity is expected, even demanded, as if it were the fixed reward of a virtuous life! How often, alas, do we find people alienated from religion because church-going or the keeping of the Commandments has not protected them from material misfortune!

But after the warning given by Christ's own lips, who can reasonably persist in so gross a distortion of our Lord's teaching? Has He not told us beforehand to anticipate trials, injustice, pain, and even death? Did He not bid us to remember His word when these things should come to pass — and, remembering it, to be comforted by the knowledge that His Spirit is with us? Yet this is precisely what we most commonly forget: the consoling truth that, despite all hardships, and amid every hardship, the heart of the faithful disciple is the abode of the Spirit of God. If we could but remember that fact constantly, then, like the martyrs of old, we would be invulnerable of soul. Nothing could hurt us; nothing could defeat us; out of every loss and every pain, we would draw occasion of new sanctity to ourselves.

It is curious that people who are familiar with the Gospel all their lives should so often forget that Christ bade His disciples to take up their cross and follow Him;[52] it is curious that Christians should so frequently cry out in protest at a little loss, or a little pain — as if Christ had represented His kingdom to be an earthly paradise! There may be men who ignore or despise the Cross, but surely this is not because Christ ignored or despised it. There may be some who refuse to practice patience in adversity, but surely this is not due to any lack of example on the part of the Christian saints.

[52] Matt. 16:24; Mark 8:34; Luke 9:23.

Be of Good Heart

The value of suffering and the worth of patience are fundamental in the teaching of Christ. Who that pays heed to Him can be unaware of that?

Another strange phenomenon is that of the Catholic Christian hearkening eagerly to a novel sect that professes to teach men how to triumph over all evil and all pain. As if Christ had not already taught that wisdom! As if that teaching had not already produced the greatest heroes and heroines of history!

God enables you to triumph over suffering

It is an old rule with the saints and their disciples that all things work together for good to those who love God.[53] It is a triumph often set down in the records of the Church that ordinary men and women have been so successfully trained to fear nothing, that they can never be robbed of joy. The teaching of Christ, as interpreted by the Church, as exemplified by the saints, has become the source of the most marvelous triumph of mind over matter. And the explanation of this perpetual miracle is to be found in the presence of the indwelling Spirit, the

[53] Rom. 8:28.

Paraclete, whom Christ sent, the Spirit who leads the disciples into all truth.[54]

Close at hand, then, in the Gospel, which is our own, in the religion that has been taught to us from the days of childhood, may be found the secret of that power which we seek in vain elsewhere. Let us not be deluded by new phrases, nor by promises wildly extravagant. Rather, let us attempt to absorb a greater share of that Christian sanctity that has brought forth such splendid fruit century after century, that eliminates evil by teaching us to cooperate with the grace of God, and that recognizes physical pain to be not a mere phantasm, but the very useful servant of the soul.

We also hear a good deal nowadays about the power of healthy thought to bring peace to the mind and strength to the body. Very often, the professed advocates of right thinking are guilty of extreme exaggeration. It is not true or reasonable to affirm that our thinking will control the whole current of events; it is not sane to hold that a right system of thought will avail to prevent all accident and all disease.

[54] John 16:13.

Be of Good Heart

The world in which we live is not the mere creation of our mind, but is the theater of events and the field of forces quite outside us and beyond our power to alter. On the other hand, it is true that the most important element in our world is the subjective element, and that no catastrophe can ever destroy the peace of the soul that lives within itself serene. We cannot say there are no misfortunes, no unhappy accidents, no undesirable and regrettable events; but we can with truth affirm that all such things may be turned to good use by the power of divine grace and the unyielding determination of the will to be loyal to God.

This is the true doctrine that our Savior taught and that the lives of Christian saints have fully and frequently demonstrated. Those who have adjusted their lives to this teaching will not be misled, nor even greatly tempted, by the extravagant promises of an untried religion that makes statements about the world and life totally at variance with reason and with common sense.

To us, then, as to the disciples on the eve of our Lord's departure, there comes the assurance, not that we shall have uninterrupted comfort, but that we shall have the assistance of the Holy Spirit to carry us through such trials as may be ours. Christ prepares us for persecution and, at the same time, promises to make us strong enough to endure and overcome.

Just as, in the history of God's saints, we perceive the realization of the divine promise of ultimate victory, so, too, we may be certain that, in our own lives, evil will never triumph, while we cling to the hand of God and follow the guidance of the Holy Spirit. For He is indeed the Paraclete, "the Comforter," in this high and holy sense. And when He has come to the soul and dwells therein, no enemy can vanquish us, no evil can really hurt us, but all things, big and little, pleasant and unpleasant, good and bad, will work together for our lasting and perfect joy.

Chapter Nine

❧

*Your Sins Can
Be Forgiven*

※

Christ calls all to repentance

We are all sinners. Men may shut their eyes to the facts confronting them; they may twist their memories and distort their judgments; they may willfully blind themselves, and externally deny the conviction forced upon their inmost souls; but they cannot look squarely at their own experiences and honestly repudiate the charge of sin. The unspoiled conscience is loud and clear in its accusation; disregarded and outraged, it will still be heard. Even in the last stage of moral callousness, a man must grip his stifled monitor by the throat, or it will rise again as from the dead and challenge him to deny his guilt.

There are kinds and degrees of sin, to be sure. There are stages in progress up toward holiness, or down toward Hell. But, one and all, we are properly classed as sinful men; the heart of every one of us yearns for reconciliation, for divine forgiveness. A sense of sin haunts the best and the worst alike; for we are, as our forefathers have been before us, and our children shall be after us. No one of us dare stand before the deep-seeing eye of God and claim to be pure. Some mercy, some purifying grace must become ours, before our hearts can ever find intimate and enduring peace.

There could be no real religion, scarcely even a pretense of religion, without the recognition of this fundamental fact and some endeavor to minister to this human need. History, when it told the story of humanity's untutored gropings after truth, and related the various human ways in which the sin-stained soul sought purgation, gave assurance thereby that in the Christian revelation there would be ample recognition of and generous provision for the sorrowful sinner.

Christ's words and deeds alike were the more-than-abundant realization of this hope. With a directness that could not be ignored, with a frequency and a wholeheartedness that scandalized the Pharisees, Christ went to the sinner and transformed his ineffectual regret into a supreme, heart-breaking grief for sin that shines out in the gospel age, and in every epoch of Christian history, as the token distinguishing the repentance of Christ's true disciples from the lip-sorrow and the half-trifling apologies of other men. He who came to minister to man's gravest needs set before us, as the very first article of His gospel, the summons to repentance and the assurance of divine pardon.[55]

Christ's Church heals the repentant sinner
As it was characteristic of Christ in His ministry, so it has been characteristic of His Church to arouse within the sorrow-stricken sinner a most undoubting conviction of forgiveness and the liveliest hope for future preservation from sin. One might be startled sometimes were it not for the plain lessons of the Gospel, and the memory of Christ's own boldness; one might be startled at the methods that the Catholic Church is wont to use in dealing with the penitent.

Unmistakable in her declaration of what God's law requires, uncompromising in the fierceness with which she denounces guilt and menaces the guilty, the Church nevertheless, with the same divine audacity that characterized our Lord, addresses sinful men with God's voice

---

[55] Cf. Matt. 4:17; Mark 1:15.

and God's authority. She ventures not only to proclaim aloud, in the world's hearing, the pardon of sin, but even to soothe and cheer the heart bruised with contrition, bidding the sinner to cast off the shameful memory and the paralyzing fear, encouraging him to stand side by side and serve on equal footing with the just who need not penance. In directness, finality, and measureless sweep, the Church's call to repent and be saved compares only with Christ's summons to prepare for the coming of the kingdom.

Human at once and Christlike, this attitude of the Church toward sin has ever been one of the strongest arguments for her divinity. It takes the experience of ages and the wisdom born of worldwide practice, it requires the tender patience of a mother and the divine love of an infinite God, thus to mingle with the offscourings of the race, to choose as a mission the treatment of all human sin, and to succeed in this ministry.

To see the Church in the fulfillment of her mission, to note her ability, her constancy, her long-suffering, her unselfishness, and her success, is to have encountered an almost irresistible appeal to accept her as divine. Where but from her teaching shall we learn skill in dealing with temptation and in curing fault? Where better than in her conduct shall we find a living example of Christ's method and of Christ's success? How many a one, drawing from afar, has known her first as the refuge of the sinner and thrown himself trustfully into her arms? Terrified by rigor, puzzled by uncertain teaching, shaken by the clash of contending systems, soul after soul, tried, tempted, fallen, all but despairing, has emerged from the strife, weary and sorely wounded. Gladly, gratefully, those souls turn toward the figure that has kept watch over humanity through the ages of its devious course, working Christ's work among men, guiding, uplifting, healing, binding up wounds that were nearly fatal, and giving new strength to undertake the struggles still to come.

It has been charged accusingly against the Church that she "hath kept company with sinners," but this is to her glory rather than to her shame. Even so did her Master, the Son of God, receive and eat with them.[56] But neither of her nor of her Founder can it be said that the work of caring for sinners made it impossible to create saints.

[56] Luke 15:2.

Be of Good Heart

As, from the same divine lips that pronounced the pardon of thief and murderer and wicked woman, there came the revelation of a spiritual ideal more divinely rav-ishing in its purity and beauty than any previously known to man, so, too, she who deserves the reproach of being the Church of sinners is likewise the fruitful mother of saints and the world's great guide and teacher of holiness. In court and camp and counting room, clad in royal robes and kitchen livery and beggars' rags, we find her holy children. There are men of genius and learning and poetic fire, alongside the ignorant and illiterate; there are statesmen, scientists, recluses, peasants, and factory girls, penitent thieves and kings and reclaimed outcasts — and to them all she holds out the guiding lamp, as they toil steadily up the heights of the sacred mountain. While she is dealing patiently with the weakest sinner and tenderly encouraging him to lift up his heart, she ever hides within her bosom the secret hope that God's mercy will yet bestow on him the grace of heroic sanctity.

For all such as are really penitent, then, no matter how scarlet their sin, nor how frequent their treason, the doctrine of the Church assures a pardon. To weak and half-blind man, as he wages inglorious war against the enemies of his own creating and goes stumbling along a road that has been broken and roughened by his own foolishness, what boon can be greater than to be sure of such an opportunity?

That every man has sinned and that even the just are never far from the danger line, makes doubly necessary the proclamation of a general forgiveness. It is not unusual for some inner convulsion of the soul to send the tide of human courage ebbing out beyond the low-water mark, or for the demon of despair to fasten grimly upon a quaking heart and make it everlastingly his own. Life is so volatile; the spirit is so delicate; men are so loath to renew the endless struggle, to hope in the face of defeat, to try and try and ever try again. Sometimes it may seem more just to be less tender with the sinner; to human wisdom, the limit of mercy appears to have been reached. But with God, with Christ, with the Church, with the Church's minister, wheresoever sin hath abounded, there doth grace superabound.[57]

As widespread as the human race and as lasting as the life of man upon earth is the Church's care of

[57] Rom. 5:20.

113

her charge. Seeking his pleasure by riotous living in a far-off country,[58] still the sinner fails to outdistance the call of her warning voice. Although he "walk in the valley of the shadow of death,"[59] he finds she has not abandoned him. Should he descend in his headlong career of wickedness to the very verge of the precipice of Hell, even there she is with him, her right hand extending the hope of pardon, her voice promising the gift of peace.

To show such inexhaustible patience toward the sinner may seem extreme; the Puritan and the Pharisee have declared it so. The Church's answer is the answer of Christ: to the lost sheep she is sent, and to those who are sick.[60] The God whose message she preaches is the God of infinite patience, and above all His other works are His tender mercies. Not to crush the bruised reed or quench the smoking flax,[61] but to kindle and fan the sacred flame of the heart's contrition — such is her mission. Although her call may fall many a time upon

[58] Luke 15:13.
[59] Ps. 22:4 (RSV = Ps. 23:4).
[60] Matt. 15:24, 9:12.
[61] Isa. 42:3.

a deafened ear and a hardened heart, yet, in the end, it may be heard and heeded, and the gain is more than the loss. God's mercy may be abused, it is true; but never is it wasted, if the sinner observes the conditions under which alone the Church promises pardon.

Forgiveness requires sincere repentance

What are these terms that are insisted upon as requisite for the forgiveness of sin? The same that Christ ever imposed, the terms given to the palsied man in the Gospel:[62] the soul that has sinned must repent.

The spirit of sorrow must descend upon the soul; grief must envelop it as a fire and kindle within its dark recesses the blaze of penitent shame. From the lips must burst forth the spontaneous cry of the stricken heart: "God, be merciful to me, a sinner!"[63] Acknowledgment of guilt in the face of the world: "Father, I have sinned against Heaven and before Thee";[64] willingness to disown and repudiate the past, to give a pledge of the future, to attempt a restoration of the ruined order and a renewal of the

[62] Matt. 9:2.
[63] Luke 18:13.
[64] Cf. Luke 15:18.

balance destroyed by sin — all this the Church insists upon as the prerequisite of that forgiveness which shall be ratified in Heaven.

Conceivably a sinner may lie to the Holy Spirit, may profess a contrition that he refuses to make interiorly his own, but such a one is surely the exception rather than the rule. He hurts himself alone, and it would not be wisdom on the part of the Church, because of him, to exclude from final forgiveness the weakling who, at last effectually repentant, comes craving pardon for the seven-times-seventieth time.[65]

Those who find it hard to see how doctrine affects conduct, or what authority has to do with moral effort, should study with care the Church's theory concerning the means and the extent of forgiveness of sin. To set before oneself a high ideal, and to labor in solitary loyalty for its attainment, is necessarily possible to only a few. The rest of us stumble and halt and go lame; we are lost without instruction and aid and encouragement. And it will be found that what men in general need most is just what the Church has to offer.

[65] Cf. Matt. 18:22.

There are countless multitudes who, but for the Church's teaching, would never have risen from their falls, nor have found again the narrow way from which, perhaps by momentary inattention, they had strayed. There have been rare and noble souls entangled in the snare of temptation, the mire of sudden sin, and the fatal quicksand of despondency, and, by the Church's aid, they have been born again to the life of saints and heroes. All such are witnesses to the divine wisdom and the divine power that reach out through the Church's instrumentality to the erring children of men. And in the same spirit and by the same authority as the Christ of the Gospels, they proclaim to the stricken of the human race: "Be of good heart: thy sins are forgiven thee."[66]

[66] Matt. 9:2.

Chapter Ten

☙

Miracles Happen

❧

Christ's miracles reveal His divine power
Frequently our Savior gave striking manifestations of His
divine power. On various occasions and in diverse ways,
He exercised His dominion over nature, suspending natural laws and delivering persons who sought His aid from
a burden of affliction. At times He went so far in the
exercise of beneficent activity as to bring people back
to life out of the very grave itself.

Although the more wonderful exhibitions of supernatural power were few, the lesser miracles were well-
nigh innumerable. Such deeds as healing the infirm of
disease, and making the lame walk, the deaf hear, and the
dumb speak seem to have been almost ordinary evidence
both of His own divine power and of His sympathy for
His Father's afflicted children.

The story of these different miracles of our Lord im-
presses us with a keen sense of the difference between
that earlier day and our own. Further, it impels many of

us to wish we had been alive in the time and place chosen by Providence for the earthly life of the Son of Man. We regret that we have missed the stimulus given to faith by miracles actually witnessed, and the stimulus given to love by miracles personally experienced.

Some of us, indeed, as we reflect on the privilege of the people who lived in Judea in that older time, are apt to feel the stirrings of a difficulty to belief, aroused by the fact that the God who was so ready with attention and so quick with aid to sufferers in those times should seem so far away and so slow to help nowadays, when we lift up unanswered prayers in the midst of trials intolerable. It is both a disappointment and an objection that the miraculous activities described in the Gospel have, in these latter days, so largely disappeared.

Christ's mission was not merely
to bestow temporal blessings

However, doubting minds must keep clearly in view the real end of our Lord's mission and the real significance of His miraculous deeds. The purpose of His coming was not mainly the bestowal of temporal blessings upon His followers, but their spiritual illumination.

Temporal blessings, it is true, were the gifts that the carnal-minded looked forward to; and failure to secure such blessings was the usual reason for our Lord's rejection by those who turned aside from Him. But if there was anything especially clear and emphatic in the doctrines of Jesus Christ, it was that His followers were to expect hardship and suffering when they undertook to follow Him. The disciples of Christ had been led to anticipate poverty and pain, and, in the subsequent course of history, actually did receive, not less, but more of it.

Although there was, so to speak, a background of miraculous relief of sufferings — as if to provide faith with a support that would endure through long ages and through violent storms — such relief was not the common experience; it was not the daily bread and meat of Christian life.

Taken all in all, grief and pain and death usually went unrelieved; the ordinary course of nature persisted; and the instances of miraculous response and interference, compared with the instances of seemingly unanswered prayer, were as millions to units. It was certainly not for the sake of bestowing material benefits that Christ came upon earth; and it was certainly not by the eager desire to witness wonders that the Christian showed himself a true disciple of his Master.

Fundamental in the religion preached by Jesus Christ is His purpose to save the spirit by the crucifixion of the flesh. No teaching could be more forcible, no example more impressive, than that which was placed irremovably before the eyes of the human race when the agony of three long hours was terminated by the dreadful death upon the Cross. Calvary gives the measure and spells out the meaning of the Christian Revelation. It blazes the way of salvation for the multitudes who are to follow with bleeding feet in the footprints of the Man of Sorrows up to the very portals of Paradise. It sets the goal of virtue and the aim of prayer in the distant shadows of the eternal years.

Not by peace and plenty upon earth is the ambition of the saint satisfied. Not in deliverance from suffering is the sure mark of divine favor found. Not in the realization of any human hope, or in the receipt of any temporal or material blessing, or in the accumulation of the goods and prizes of this present life, does the Christian find his reward. Rather are Christ's followers to be recognized as truly His by their patient endurance of suffering, their spirit of renunciation, and their ready abandonment of the present for the sake of the future.

Visible blessings bestowed on us come, as it were, by chance, and indirectly; we have received no pledge or promise with regard to them. Whether this or that gift would tend to our good or ill is oftentimes a secret known only to God, and we dare not ask for it except with the reservation that it be withheld if incompatible with God's purpose.

But at least we may be infallibly sure that the faithful following of the Master's will must ultimately meet with reward — a reward exceedingly great, beyond all human power to estimate, as enduring and everlasting as God Himself. It is for the sake of a return such as this that wisdom bids us renounce the things of earth, and abandon private, selfish, sinful aims absolutely and forever.

This great lesson on the supreme aspiration of man and the divinely appointed means for its attainment, Christ taught clearly during the short span of years that He dwelt visibly here. Having planted the tiny mustard seed, He withdrew, leaving to men its cultivation. Gradually the centuries unfold its possibilities; gradually it is

transformed into the mighty, visible kingdom of God.[67]
One after another, the early promises are realized; one
after another, Christ's words and principles are under-
stood in their profounder meaning.

The greater miracles are those that touch the soul

So, too, as the individual Christian advances in the
life of virtue, he appreciates the value of the spiritual
over the material. More and more he perceives that the
temporal blessings bestowed by Christ upon His own
generation were but little things when compared with
the spiritual gifts bestowed upon the Church, to be by
her in turn imparted to men until the end of time.

Thus it is with the miracles related in the Gospel.
That a dumb man's tongue should be loosed and the gift
of speech be received by one who had never uttered an
articulate sound was a wonder great enough to excite the
marvel of the people, and significant enough to deserve
to be recorded by the Evangelist.[68] But the man who stud-
ies the result of Christianity upon human conduct as a

[67] Matt. 13:31-32.
[68] Matt. 9:33; Luke 11:14.

whole, or who appreciates the influence of Christ's grace upon the inner life of his own conscience, will quickly understand that greater miracles than giving speech to the dumb are daily recorded in the long story of God's gracious dealings with the souls our Savior redeemed.

In all ages and among all races, the deaf have been made to hear and the dumb to speak. Men who were as stones in their irresponsiveness, who would turn away from the message of an angel, who seemed destined to remain criminal and heedless until death — men like these have been made to hear and to obey the gentle persuasion of the Savior's voice. They have grown, by His miraculous healing, sensitive beyond belief to the slightest whispers of the Holy Spirit, docile and zealous in the performance of every sort of unselfish and virtuous deed.

Surely it is no less a miracle to give hearing to the soul than to the flesh; it is more of a blessing that a hardened sinner should become heedful of God's warning voice than that his ears should be unstopped. The power to hear physical sounds is a lesser gift, and its bestowal upon a man born deaf is a lesser wonder than the grace given to a vicious spirit, wrapped in the bondage of sin and deafened by the loud noise of worldly pleasure, when such a one is led to understand and adopt the most lofty and heroic ideals the mind of man has ever known. Who that reads a little of the history of Christ's grace will deny that miracles like these happen over and over again in this very day and this very land in which we live?

And then there are the dumb who are made to speak. That to a grown man there should be given or restored the faculty of speech is without doubt a marvel. But that tongues and lips that never uttered anything but foulness and blasphemy should be converted into organs through which the Spirit of God discourses heavenly music — this indeed, beyond question, would be a greater miracle.

Yet we know (many of us by immediate experience) that, in this sense, too, God's grace is wonderfully active. Those who scoffed have learned to pray. They who were the promoters and the propagandists of awful wickedness have become the messengers of Christ's glad tidings and the zealous preachers of the grace of God. It is among the most evident proofs of the Church's divine origin that so often, by means of her sacraments, healing graces such as these are distributed to the wretched children of men.

There is, then, no lack of opportunity for us who live at this long distance of time from Christ's own generation. We have, if we will but examine it, strong evidence of His beneficent activity and His divine power here among us, day after day.

We ourselves may become recipients of His healing, soothing, uplifting grace; we may win His blessings for those needy ones who are dear to us; we may help the deaf to hear with distinctness, and the dumb to speak sweetly and clearly. Often, as we stand near and watch, Christ raises the dead to life. The wonders we see may not be done in the same fashion as the wonders of the Gospel; but they are nonetheless marvelous and nonetheless true.

Learn to appreciate the spiritual
gifts God bestows on you

It becomes us not therefore, to dream of what might have been, had we lived in another age and another place. Rather, let us make ourselves familiar with and responsive to our own opportunities. Otherwise we shall miss the greater gifts, while wishing idly for the lesser. Here and now, amid the circumstances where our lot is cast by Providence, our chance of Heaven must be sought; it is the graces actually offered us that present our best possibility of perfection.

Those of us who are wise, then, will make much of our actual spiritual privileges. Instead of regretting that Christ's visible presence is no longer continued here upon earth, we shall open our eyes to gifts bestowed upon us that are greater than the gift of Christ's visible presence. Calling upon Him to open our spiritual eyes, and unlock our souls' tongues, and unstop the deafness of our spirits, we shall surely receive from Him the grace that most we need. Having corresponded with the given help, we shall achieve wondrous results.

And at last we shall come to understand that we missed no supreme blessing by being born just when and where we have been born, or by being placed in circumstances which actually make up our lot. God's grace, united with our efforts, will carry us happily to our destiny. And, from the gates of eternity, we shall look back with gladness upon the days and the conditions of our earthly life, and bear witness to His wisdom and His goodness, crying out joyfully, "He hath done all things well."[69]

[69] Mark 7:37.

Biographical Note

❧

Joseph McSorley
(1874-1963)

❧

Born in Brooklyn, New York, Joseph McSorley was edu-
cated at St. John's Preparatory School and St. John's Col-
lege, from which he graduated at the early age of sixteen.
At only twenty-two, he was ordained a priest in the
Paulist order, having received special permission because
of his young age. After serving as a priest in Washington
and New York for several years and as an army chaplain
for a brief time, Fr. McSorley became superior general of
the Paulists, a position he held from 1924 until 1929.
While he was superior general, the order established a
Catholic radio station. In 1932, Fr. McSorley became a
contributing editor of *The Catholic World*.

Fr. McSorley authored and translated several books,
wrote numerous doctrinal and devotional pamphlets
and articles, and contributed entries to the *Catholic Ency-
clopedia*. A zealous priest and popular retreat master,
preacher, and lecturer, he directed all the souls in his care
with kindness and understanding. His own hopeful spirit,

grounded solidly in God's promises, shines through in his engaging writing style and in his inspiring words that invite all Christians to rejoice in the great hope to which we are called.

✧

Sophia Institute is a nonprofit institution that seeks to restore man's knowledge of eternal truth, including man's knowledge of his own nature, his relation to other persons, and his relation to God.

Sophia Institute Press® serves this end in numerous ways. It publishes translations of foreign works to make them accessible for the first time to English-speaking readers. It brings back into print books that have long been out of print. And it publishes important new books that fulfill the ideals of Sophia Institute. These books afford readers a rich source of the enduring wisdom of mankind.

Sophia Institute Press® makes these high-quality books available to the general public by using advanced technology and by soliciting donations to subsidize its general publishing costs. Your generosity can help Sophia Institute Press® to provide the public with editions of works containing the enduring wisdom of the ages.

Please send your tax-deductible contribution to the address below. We also welcome your questions, comments, and suggestions.

For your free catalog, call:
Toll-free: 1-800-888-9344

or write:
Sophia Institute Press®
Box 5284, Manchester, NH 03108

or visit our website:
www.sophiainstitute.com

3 5282 00595 4360